Inventors and Artists

Program Authors

Connie Juel, Ph.D.

Jeanne R. Paratore, Ed.D.

Deborah Simmons, Ph.D.

Sharon Vaughn, Ph.D.

W9-AGP-770

PEARSON
Scott
Foresman

Glenview, Illinois
Boston, Massachusetts
Chandler, Arizona
Upper Saddle River, New Jersey

ISBN-13: 978-0-328-45294-1
ISBN-10:   0-328-45294-7

8 9 10 V011 14 13
CC1

UNIT 3
Inventors and Artists

Inventors and Inventions 5

How can we use our imaginations to invent?

Art and Artists 31

What is art?

Inventors and Inventions

Inventors and Inventions

Let's Explore

Choose an activity about this week's concept—Inventors and Inventions!

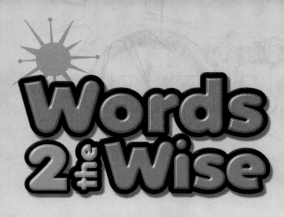

Words 2 the Wise

The smallest problems can lead to the greatest inventions. As you read, think about how these **inventors and inventions** help solve problems.

Let's Explore Famous Inventions

Inventors see ideas that others don't see. Imagine a robot small enough to crawl through pipes. It can check for leaking chemicals. It can sneak under doors.

Inventors did imagine it. They made a tiny robot vehicle that is smaller than a cherry. Inventors plan to attach a tiny camera to it next.

What else might it do?

This foldable scooter was invented in Taiwan. Gino Tsai (SY) wanted a way to get around his factory floors faster.

Stephanie Kwolek invented a fiber that police officers can use to stop bullets.

Marconi listened to this machine to hear radio messages from across the Atlantic Ocean in 1901.

Can a fiber, or cloth, stop bullets? Stephanie Kwolek (KWOH-lek) invented a fiber that does. Now her invention is used in bulletproof vests and helmets.

Guglielmo Marconi (goo-lee-EL-moh mar-KOHN-ee) thought he could use radio waves so that people could communicate across the Atlantic Ocean. Few believed him, but he was successful!

INVENTED
by Love

by John Manos

illustrated by Bill Petersen

Inventors all see a need that their new product, or invention, will answer. But *why* do they do it?

Some inventors want to make money. Others just like to experiment. They test one idea after another. It is like play for them.

And some inventors are moved by love. This was true of Kyle Power of Methuen (meth-YOO-in), Massachusetts. Kyle's five-year-old sister, Casey, had difficulty walking. Her leg muscles were weak, and she had trouble keeping her balance.

Kyle Power's invention helped his sister, Casey, walk better.

Casey would walk across pillows to strengthen her leg muscles and help improve her balance.

Casey's fifth-grade brother had a better idea. Kyle designed small wooden platforms* with adjustable straps. Casey could attach them to her shoes.

Kyle made his platforms so that different bottoms could be added. The attachments hold different-sized balls. Kyle had to experiment with several different balls and glues. He couldn't just nail the balls to the boards.

*platforms flat, raised surfaces

Kyle invented platforms that could attach to Casey's shoes.

11

The platforms were ready for Casey! The platforms made her muscles stronger and improved her coordination. Kyle called his invention "Casey Coordinators." But his invention did not just appear from thin air.

How Kyle Got Started

Kyle's school was getting ready for the Fifth Grade Invention Convention. He decided to enter the platforms into the convention.

Kyle won first place in the Invention Convention. The school then entered the "Casey Coordinators" in the 2004 Invent America! competition.

The "Casey Coordinators" won first place at Kyle's school competition.

What Is Invent America?

Invent America! began in 1987. It is a contest for students from kindergarten through eighth grade. Students sign up online. Invent America! sends a handbook with instructions. The handbook guides teachers and students from start to finish.

Invent America! knows that inventors need to follow a process. What is this step-by-step process?

- Inventors discover a problem.

- They form a theory, or an idea they can test, about how the problem might be solved.

- Inventors brainstorm and consider possible solutions.

- Inventors evaluate each solution and decide on one.

- Inventors experiment and draw the invention.

- Inventors explain the invention.

Invent America! provides young inventors with the tools they need to prepare their entries for the contest.

The Inventor's Log

Invent America! sends an Inventor's Log to everyone who enters the contest. Students use it during each step of the process.

Inventors brainstorm lots of ideas. They consider any idea that might work. They can record ideas in the log.

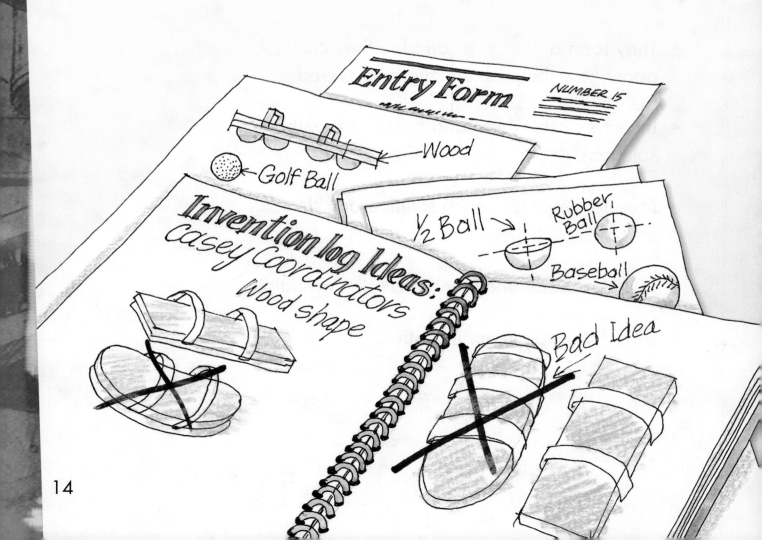

Inventors do research to learn how other people might have solved the same problems. They write notes about the research in logs.

What will the new invention look like? Inventors draw sketches in logs. They also record their experiments in logs.

Kyle's theory was that the platforms could take the place of cushions for Casey. He thought the balls beneath her feet would help her concentrate on her balance. He was right!

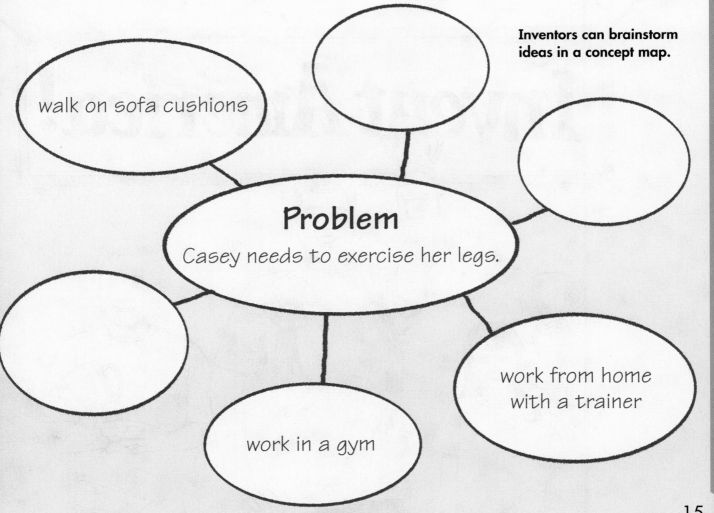

Inventors can brainstorm ideas in a concept map.

walk on sofa cushions

Problem
Casey needs to exercise her legs.

work in a gym

work from home with a trainer

How the Contest Is Judged

Invent America! evaluates inventions and chooses winners. The Invent America! judges evaluate students' drawings, theories, and research. Finally, the judges decide which inventions are the most creative and the most useful.

Student inventors can win U.S. Savings Bonds in an Invent America! contest. The winning inventions may be displayed at the Smithsonian Institution in Washington, D.C.

One young inventor traveled to Japan to accept an award. Others have received congratulations from the President of the United States and have appeared on television shows.

How Kyle's Story Ends

Kyle's "Casey Coordinators" won third place in the 2004 Invent America! contest. Kyle was on national TV. He was also honored at a Boston Celtics basketball game!

What did Kyle say after more than 14,000 people cheered for him in the basketball stadium? "It was cool."

Kyle Power was honored during halftime at a Boston Celtics basketball game.

What Do You Think?

What are the steps in the process of making an invention?

The *Cool* Invention

by Mark Rafenstein

illustrated by Bradley Clark

Celia (SEAL-yuh) is a brilliant young girl. Her mind never seems to rest. It is as if it's always running, trying to reach a finish line.

Celia is also a bookworm. Her favorite books tell about inventions. She gobbles up these books as if they were tasty treats.

Last week Celia decided to put some of her ideas to work. And that is when all the trouble began!

It was the middle of summer.
Celia noticed that her dog, Sheba
(SHEE-buh), wouldn't play. She
would just lie around and pant.

She must be hot, Celia thought.
How can I help her? What can I invent?

An idea flashed in Celia's mind.
"I have it!" she shouted to Sheba.
"Wait here."

In twenty minutes, Celia came back. She had an umbrella, a pony saddle, and some rope.

"Don't worry," Celia told her. "Soon you will be cool as ice."

Sheba sat quietly. First Celia carefully strapped the saddle on her back.

Then she placed the umbrella through a hole in the saddle. Finally she opened the umbrella.

"Now you will be shaded from the sun, Sheba," Celia said. "That should keep you cool."

Sheba went wild! First she tried to get the saddle off with her paws. Then she spun around in circles trying to shake it off. Finally she began running as fast as she could.

Sheba flew around the backyard, flinging grass and dirt everywhere. Then she raced around the patio knocking down plants and chairs. The entire backyard was a mess.

Just then, Celia's parents came home. "What happened?" Celia's mom asked.

"Well, umm, my invention failed," Celia answered.

Her parents calmed down after Celia explained everything.

"I know you were trying to help Sheba," Dad told her. "But you could have hurt her. Next time you should consider such things."

He was right. "That was my first and *last* invention," Celia told herself.

That night she could not sleep.

The next day she went to her summer science class. She was very sleepy.

Mr. Mueller (MYOOL-er), Celia's teacher, noticed. "Are you bored?" he asked.

"No, just tired." Then Celia told him why. "My last invention was a disaster. I'm done inventing, Mr. Mueller," she said.

"Done after one try?" he asked. Then he gave her a book about Samuel Morse, a great inventor.

"Read chapter 5 first," said Mr. Mueller.

Celia read that many of Morse's inventions did not work right away. He had to work many years on some of them.

The next day another idea flashed in her mind. Celia ran to explain her brilliant idea to Dad.

Celia and Dad went into the garage. They searched around for an old fan. They finally found one.

They put new batteries in the fan. Then they found an old coat hook.

Next they drilled a small hole in the side of Sheba's doghouse. Then they hung the hook from the hole. Finally, they hung the fan from the hook.

"Sheba, get in your house," ordered Celia. "Dad, turn on the fan, please!"

Soon Celia shouted, "Look! It works! Sheba is smiling!"

The invention was brilliant. And it was only Celia's second try!

What Do You Think?

What steps did Celia and Dad take to make her final invention?

Perfectly WACKY Inventions

Not all inventions become famous.
Some are just plain wacky!

Automatic Foot Warmer

Just breathe into the funnel as you walk.
Your warm breath travels down tubes
and into your shoes. Now your feet
will stay warm!

Chewing Gum Locket

Not done with your chewing gum? Put it
inside this locket and save it for later! You
can keep your chewing gum locket in your
pocket or wear it around your neck.

Animal Ear Protectors

These keep your dog's ears from falling in its food. Chow time!

An Overcoat for Two People

This overcoat starts as a coat for one person. Then it can expand. You can invite a friend to keep warm with you!

An Anti-Accident Device

A gadget on the front and rear of a car is covered with pillows or thick blankets. A person who bumps into it will just feel the soft padding.

A Mechanical Golf Instructor

Your feet are strapped into plates. Your waist is in a belt. Your head and chin are strapped inside a cap. Your golf club is attached to a machine. The machine guides your body as it moves the club!

A Swimming Device

Strap into this rubber device that is inflated with air. Sit upright in the water. Steer with the handle that's attached. Swimming is easy!

Umbrella Tube

If an umbrella doesn't keep you dry in a windy rain, try using an umbrella tube. Just attach this drop-down tube to your umbrella!

Butter Stick

Can't seem to spread butter evenly on your toast? Use a butter stick. You won't need a knife!

Ever-ready Tissues

Do you always run out of tissues when you have a cold? Attach this tissue dispenser to your head. You'll always be ready for the next sneeze.

4 You 2 Do

Word Play

Play a guessing game with each of the highlighted vocabulary words. Don't say the word aloud. Instead, choose one of these ways to give hints.

- Tell what it is not.
- Tell what it means.
- Give examples or act it out.

Then let others guess the word.

Making Connections

How are the steps that inventors take similar to the ones Celia took? How are they different?

On Paper

If you could create an invention, what would it be? Describe it.

Art and Artists

Contents

Art and Artists

Words 2 the Wise

We are surrounded by art everywhere we go. As you read, think about what you know about **art and artists.**

Art

Art is not only in museums. It is on the sidewalk. It shoots high up into the sky. It is made of tiny pieces of colored glass. It entertains us in the Sunday newspaper.

Every person might not enjoy the same types of art. Some people might think certain examples of art are beautiful. Others might disagree.

Can a rocking horse be art? This wooden rocking horse is an example of folk art.

Artists create art in many different ways. An artist can use media (MEE-dee-uh) such as chalk, paint, clay, glass, or canvas. Different styles of art are all around us. The words *folk, abstract,* and *realistic* describe some art styles.

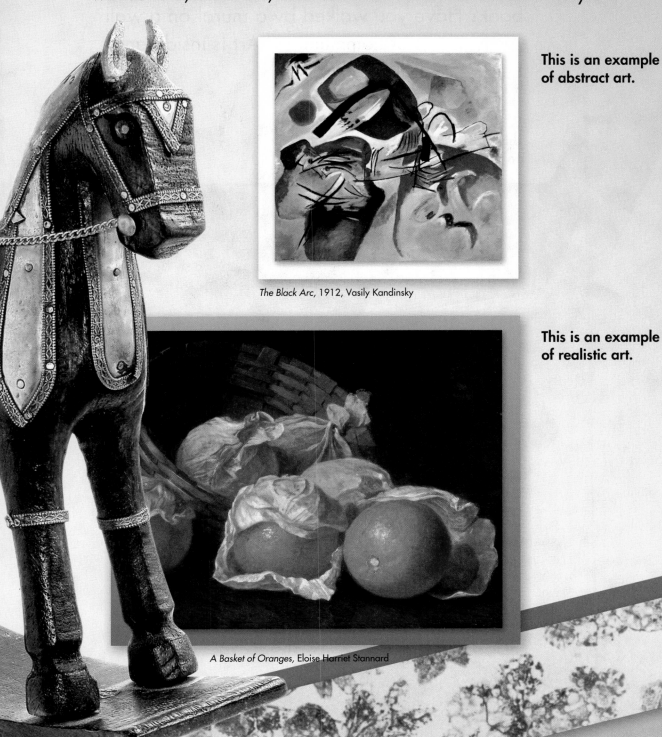

This is an example of abstract art.

The Black Arc, 1912, Vasily Kandinsky

This is an example of realistic art.

A Basket of Oranges, Eloise Harriet Stannard

Have you ever noticed a fancy arch above a doorway? Have you ever looked at a comic book? Have you walked by a mural on a wall? Art is a part of communities. Art is inside and outside of buildings.

This artist creates his work on a busy city sidewalk.

Look for art that makes you stop and say, "I like it!"

Is it from the past, or is it modern? Is it painted like a photograph, or are the colors and shapes more like a dream? The art you like tells something about you!

Yellow and Gold, Mark Rothko

Could you pass Mark Rothko's painting without stopping to look at its colors?

This bean-shaped sculpture in Chicago's Millennium Park is called *Cloud Gate.*

ART

Is Everywhere

by Robert Kausal

Where would you go in your community to see art? How about a museum? There are thousands of museums in the United States! Many of these are art museums. They display collections of paintings, sculptures, photographs, and much more. Some museums even have furniture that is art!

Museums help us learn about our history. And they inspire us with new ideas. Millions of people in this country visit museums each year.

The Metropolitan Museum of Art in New York City has the largest collection of art in the country. At this museum you can see art from ancient civilizations and by modern-day artists.

Some of the world's most famous art is displayed at the Metropolitan. Vincent van Gogh's painting called *Sunflowers* is displayed there. Look at the picture at the top of the page. What do you see in the painting?

Vincent van Gogh taught himself to draw and paint. He painted *Sunflowers* in 1887.

Sunflowers, 1887, Vincent van Gogh

The Metropolitan is the largest museum in New York City.

The Art Institute of Chicago also has many paintings that capture scenes from real life. One of the museum's most famous paintings is *Nighthawks* by Edward Hopper. He painted it after visiting a restaurant in New York City.

Art can also make us think. The Art Institute has a painting by René Magritte called *Time Transfixed.* It shows a train speeding out of a fireplace. Sometimes art seems more like a dream.

Art can make us think. What does this painting called *Time Transfixed* make you think about?

Time Transfixed, 1938, René Magritte

Edward Hopper painted *Nighthawks* in 1942. Why do you think he called it *Nighthawks?*

Nighthawks, 1942, Edward Hopper

Alma Thomas was a teacher for thirty-five years before becoming a full-time artist.

Mike Fischer, *Portrait of Alma Woodsey Thomas in Front of Her Work* (1976), Smithsonian American Art Museum, Washington, D.C.

This painting by Alma Thomas shows her colorful style.

Alma Woodsey Thomas, *The Eclipse* (1970), Smithsonian American Art Museum, Washington, D.C.

Many artists are famous because of their style of painting. Alma Thomas is known for her use of color in her paintings. She paints patterns with bright colors. You can see many of her paintings at the Smithsonian American Art Museum.

After visiting an art museum, you might want to start working on your own art. But where else can you go to see and learn about art?

Does your community have an art gallery? Many art galleries hire professional artists. They can teach you how to express yourself in different styles using many different methods.

You can learn how to paint. But you can also learn ceramics, animation, film, and even computer art. Galleries give you the opportunity to display or perform your art for the community.

In Chicago, Gallery 37 has been doing just that since 1991.

Many communities in America have art galleries.

Gallery 37 Center for the Arts may not look like much from the outside, but inside there is a lot going on. The gallery has five floors of activities. Besides teaching painting, sculpting, and ceramics, the gallery also teaches radio, film, dance, music, and much more.

Gallery 37 encourages young people to express their creativity. The goal at Gallery 37 is not just to show your work in the gallery, but also to share it with the community.

Many communities offer art classes for young people.

You don't just find art in museums and art galleries. Many communities also display public art. Sometimes it is murals. These are large colorful paintings on walls. Sometimes it is a famous architect's building. And sometimes it is a herd of cows.

In 1999 Chicago displayed 300 life-sized cows throughout the downtown area. Artists, architects, photographers, and even some celebrities individually designed each cow. The art exhibit was a big success.

"Cows on Parade" in downtown Chicago

The "Cows on Parade" art exhibit was such a big hit in Chicago that many other cities followed with their own cow parades.

Public displays of art aren't just for tourists. They also help the community and the world. Art helps us express who we are. Look around your community. Art is everywhere!

What Do You Think?

Why is art so important to a community?

Community Art

by Elizabeth Brennan

Art Speaks

Some artists paint on canvas. Community artists use their communities as their canvases. Their art may be on an outdoor wall, in a garden, or on a bench. Other community members share their talents too. They may put on a play or a concert. They use their talents to make their neighborhoods beautiful and enjoyable.

Community art projects bring artists of all ages together. Everyone can be proud of seeing his or her neighbors' creativity.

Without Permission

Many young people look for ways to express themselves. Some write on public spaces like desks, walls, or trains. They do this without the community's permission. This is a crime. These young people may be arrested or pay fines. Many times, the judge makes them use their talents for good.

Community artists of all ages want to express themselves in beautiful ways. Where can they find a place to create art?

Community members work to keep the community beautiful.

Some communities hire artists to paint something beautiful in public places. It becomes outdoor art. But community artists have other reasons to create art.

Art 180

Art 180 is an organization in Richmond, Virginia. It gives kids the chance to express themselves through community art. It challenges young people to talk about important topics. First, children discuss their ideas. Then they paint, write, or create art. This art expresses how they feel about these topics.

Art allows artists to express who they are.

I'm MORE Than what You make Me to Be.

A message from Tasha and Dee Dee, sponsored by Weed & Seed and ART 180.

A member of Art 180 paints a self-portrait on a mirror.

Children used an Art 180 project, Gilpin Garden, to speak out against crime in their community. They painted wooden flowers and attached them to the metal fence around their buildings. It made the fence look cheerful. It showed community pride.

Some fifth grade artists painted pictures of themselves. They used mirrors as a medium for their self-portraits. Then their work became the "Wall of Mirrors." Visitors from the community came to admire the wall.

This is only the bottom section of the art students' 20-foot mural in Harrisburg, Pennsylvania!

Mural Arts Program

Philadelphia has a Mural Arts Program. The program teaches people how to paint murals. Professional artists give advice to beginning artists in the community.

Artists tell what happens in their communities. They tell its hopes too. They use murals to tell the story.

Other children in Pennsylvania worked on a mural outside the Department of Education building. They believe that you never stop learning. This belief shows in the mural.

Community Performance Art

Artists can also be performers. The talents of performers make a community better too. Some children have acting, singing, or dancing talent. The Boston Children's Museum has a program called Friday Night Lights. The show features local youths. Dancers, actors, and singers of all ages can use the professional stage at the museum.

These dancers make art their own in *The Harlem Nutcracker.*

Agnes Denes's art was a wheat field in the city.

Creative People and Their Projects

Agnes Denes (DEN-eez) planted two acres of wheat on an empty lot in New York City. Imagine golden wheat waving back and forth in the middle of a city! The field was her artwork, and it said that the empty lot wasted the land.

Joseph Beuys (bois) planted 7,000 trees throughout the city of Kassel, Germany. It made the city more beautiful. This artist was saying, "Make your city beautiful."

Young Artists Around the World

Many nations have projects that support community art. In Ireland and the United Kingdom, young students publish their writings in an online magazine. Some perform with the Rock Festival Group. Others act in films to speak out for children's rights. These projects were started by the Carnegie Young People Initiative.

What important message do you have? Are creative ideas springing up right now? You might be ready to get involved in a community art project!

Art is what you decide it is.

What Do You Think?

How can artists express themselves in a community?

The Paint Box

By E.V. Rieu

"Cobalt and umber and ultramarine,
Ivory black and emerald green—
What shall I paint to give pleasure to you?"
"Paint for me somebody utterly new."

"Now mix me a color that nobody knows,
And paint me a country where nobody goes.
And put in it people a little like you,
Watching a unicorn drinking the dew."

Genius

By Nikki Grimes

"Sis! Wake up!" I whisper
in the middle of the night.

Urgently, I shake her
till she switches on the light.

The spiral notebook in my hand
provides her quick relief.

It tells her there's no danger
of a break-in by a thief.

"Okay," she says, then, props herself
up vertically in bed.

She nods for me to read my work.
I cough, then forge ahead.

The last verse of my poem leaves
her silent as a mouse.

I worry till she says, "We have
a genius in the house."

4 you 2 Do

Word Play

Match these words to their meanings.

canvas   mural   gallery   express

1. This is a surface on which artists can paint.
2. This means "to show."
3. This is a place where art is displayed.
4. This is a painting the size of a wall.

Making Connections

How is art in museums like community art? How is it different?

On Paper

Do you like to paint, draw, or write? Tell how you like to express yourself.

Answers to Word Play
1. canvas; 2. express;
3. gallery; 4. mural

Digging Dino

Contents

Digging Dino

Words 2 the Wise

Paleontologists dig dinosaur bones to learn about the past. As you read, think about what you know about **dinosaurs and paleontology.**

Let's Explore
EXCAVATION

Hadrosaurus was a plant-eating dinosaur.

Before the 1800s, people thought dinosaurs might not have really existed. Then paleontologists found some large lizard-like bones. Paleontologists are scientists who study fossils and prehistoric life.

But without a full set of bones, the puzzle was incomplete. In 1858, paleontologists discovered a whole prehistoric skeleton, and they named it *Hadrosaurus*. They proved that dinosaurs had existed!

One of the most amazing discoveries happened in 1990. Paleontologists excavated a *Tyrannosaurus rex* and found nearly every bone! Its name means "Tyrant Lizard King." This dinosaur is also called T-Rex.

The T-Rex skeleton was named Sue. Sue lived more than 67 million years ago. T-Rex Sue is named after the paleontologist, Sue Hendrickson, who discovered it.

Paleontologists find treasures that help explain the prehistoric past!

Snap! With jaws this size, meat-eating Sue ate every bite.

TREASURE

by Marcus Brett

Paleontologists are treasure hunters. But they don't hunt for gold. They hunt for a different treasure. Paleontologists are scientists who hunt for fossils. Fossils, such as bones, are clues to prehistoric life.

Sometimes paleontologists are on the hunt for months. And they might not find a single fossil. Other times, they strike it rich! They discover sites that hold lots of fossils. Paleontologists excavate, or dig up, these sites. They learn new and surprising information about prehistoric animals.

Paleontologists uncover a giant dinosaur called *Titanosaurus*.

HUNTERS

Trapped in Oil

Oil rests deep in the Earth's crust. In some places the oil seeps to the surface. When oil hits air, it gets thick and sticky. This sticky oil is called tar. In Rancho La Brea (RAN-cho lah-BRAY-uh), California, tar has been collecting in pools for 40,000 years.

Early explorers to California found animal bones sticking out of these tar pools. They thought the bones belonged to cattle. Then in 1901, paleontologists started to look more closely at the bones.

The La Brea Tar Pits in California hold the bones of extinct animals.

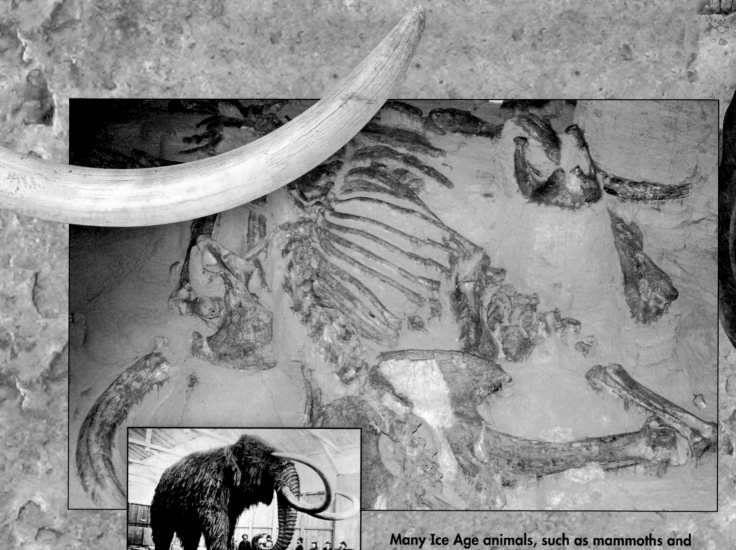

Many Ice Age animals, such as mammoths and saber-toothed cats, visited the La Brea Tar Pits and were trapped in tar.

These scientists discovered that the bones belonged to extinct animals. These animals wandered this area during the Ice Age! They became trapped in the tar. The animals died, but the bones remained. The tar kept them hard. Over time the bones became fossils.

For over one hundred years, paleontologists have been excavating fossils from the La Brea Tar Pits. They now have over three million fossils! They've even dug up bones of huge creatures, such as mammoths and mastodons (MAS-tuh-dahns)!

They've discovered bones from fierce hunters, such as saber-toothed cats and American lions. They've even discovered bones from an extinct camel!

Follow the Footprints

Bones like the ones found at La Brea are fossils. Old, hardened animal footprints are also fossils. Paleontologists can learn from studying these footprints too.

Large footprints such as these are some of the most common tracks found along old shores.

One hundred million years ago, a great sea covered much of North America. When animals walked along the shore, they left footprints in the sand. Over time the sand hardened into sandstone. Other layers of stone covered the sandstone.

Later, wind and rain washed away some of the stone to reveal the tracks again. The most common track belonged to a duck-billed dinosaur. Paleontologists have discovered many of these fossils along what was once the shore of this sea.

Dinosaur Freeway runs
for hundreds of miles
through New Mexico
and Colorado.

Many of the tracks are side by side. Scientists
think these clues mean that many dinosaurs traveled
in herds. Paleontologists have a theory that these
dinosaurs migrated, or moved from one area to another.
Paleontologists named this migration path "Dinosaur
Freeway."

An Egg-citing Discovery

Fossils of baby dinosaurs are a rare treasure. This
is because the bones of baby dinosaurs were very soft.

Fossils of dinosaur babies like the ones found at Auca Mahuevo are very rare.

Soft bones don't become fossils easily. But in 1997 paleontologists made a rare discovery.

At Auca Mahuevo (OW-kuh mah-WAY-voh), Argentina, paleontologists discovered a dinosaur nesting ground. This site held hundreds of titanosaur (ty-TAN-o-sawr) eggs. Titanosaur was a large plant-eating dinosaur. The titanosaur eggs were buried in a mudflow. This stopped the eggs from decaying. Inside some of these eggs were the fossils of baby dinosaurs. Some eggs even held bits of dinosaur skin!

The dinosaur skin found in some of the eggs at Auca Mahuevo was scaly like a lizard's skin.

Paleontologists were able to prove that the titanosaur laid eggs. Now, they had an idea of what baby titanosaurs looked like.

The Hunt Continues

The La Brea Tar Pits, Dinosaur Freeway, and Auca Mahuevo are three sites with many fossils. There are many other sites around the world. Some haven't even been discovered yet! Paleontologists will keep hunting for these treasures. It's their mission to dig up the past. The fossils they find will tell us more about prehistoric times.

What Do You Think?

How do paleontologists learn about prehistoric times?

What a Find!

by Clare O'Brien   illustrated by K.E. Lewis

Before I tell you the story of my discovery, there's one thing you should know about me, Maxwell Vargas. I love dinosaurs!

By the time I was a kindergartener, I knew all of the names of dinosaurs. By second grade, I could even spell their names!

In third grade, I cornered people and told them facts, like not all dinosaurs were huge. The smallest dinosaur was about the size of a chicken.

Anyway, now I'm in fifth grade, and I usually keep my dinosaur interest to myself. But then I saw a news report . . .

A kid who lived about 12 miles away, named Sam, was being interviewed. He was helping dig up weeds in the garden, and guess what? He found a prehistoric fossil! I have dreamed of doing that since I was five! Life just isn't fair.

As you can imagine, I was pretty upset about this. Then I decided to take action. A paleontologist can't sit still when there are dinosaur bones to find!

So I got out my tools and began digging in my backyard. The holes drove my parents crazy, but they knew how important this was to me. So they let me dig.

My dog, Sparky, is a good digger, and I hoped his nose would lead us to something big.

When I was digging, I discovered all kinds of things. I found large rocks, old toys, and even a pile of chicken bones. But I didn't find a single fossil!

One day while we worked, Sparky raced into the yard dragging something big in his mouth. He dropped it at my feet. It was a huge bone! This had to be another prehistoric find!

I wondered how old it was and what animal it came from.

I measured the bone. Then I looked in a book about dinosaurs. On one page the bone matched a bone in the picture. The bone looked just like the thigh bone, or femur (FEE-mur), of a *Tyrannosaurus rex.*

I didn't waste any time! I had been pen pals with Dr. Angela Sato (SAH-toe), a paleontologist, since my third grade field trip to the Natural Science Museum.

I called Dr. Sato. She said she'd come right over. The next thing I knew, Dr. Sato, Sparky, and I had made fossil history!

Over the next weeks Dr. Sato's crew dug up my yard and our neighbor's yard. There wasn't just one bone. There was a whole skeleton! It was a nearly complete mastodon skeleton. The fossils were at least 30,000 years old!

The town newspaper printed an article about our adventures. There was a picture of Sparky and me with the mastodon bone we found.

Dr. Sato's crew was busy assembling the skeleton at the museum. She invited me to come to the museum after school to help. I cleaned bones with tiny brushes. We took photos for the museum's Web site. Then Dr. Sato told me the best news of all.

I got to name the skeleton! All of the skeletons on display have scientific names and names that give them a personality. Some skeletons are named for the paleontologists who discovered them. That's why Dr. Sato asked me!

I thought "Sparky" might be a good name for the mastodon I found in my backyard. Dr. Sato and the crew did too!

'SPARKY'
MAMMUT AMERICANUM

What Do You Think?

Why did Maxwell and Dr. Sato become pen pals?

T-Rex SPEAKS

Psst! Hey, you!

Yeah, I'm talking to you. I see you staring at my steak-knife teeth. You think I look tough now? Well, you should've seen me back in my day!

I'm talking 65 million years ago. Back when the world was one warm, giant jungle. I was the Lizard King!

Believe me, you would NOT want to get in my way! I could've eaten you and seven of your friends in one bite!

Lucky for your species* there weren't any humans in *my* kingdom. Besides, I'd much prefer to sink my teeth into a tasty *Triceratops*.

Speaking of feasting, you know those nosy bone-diggers are still trying to figure out how I snagged my meals.

Some say I was a hunter. Others think I sniffed out leftovers. Well, I'm not one to give secrets away, but let's just say I didn't starve.

*species certain kind or sort

Ah, you're admiring my two-clawed arms and big, long tail?

When I had all my muscles, I could swat ten elephants across this room with my tail. And no, I'm not telling you how I used my arms. If those fossil-hunters can't figure it out, then I'm keeping my five-foot-long jaw closed!

You want to know how dinosaurs became extinct? I hate to break it to you, but I have no idea.

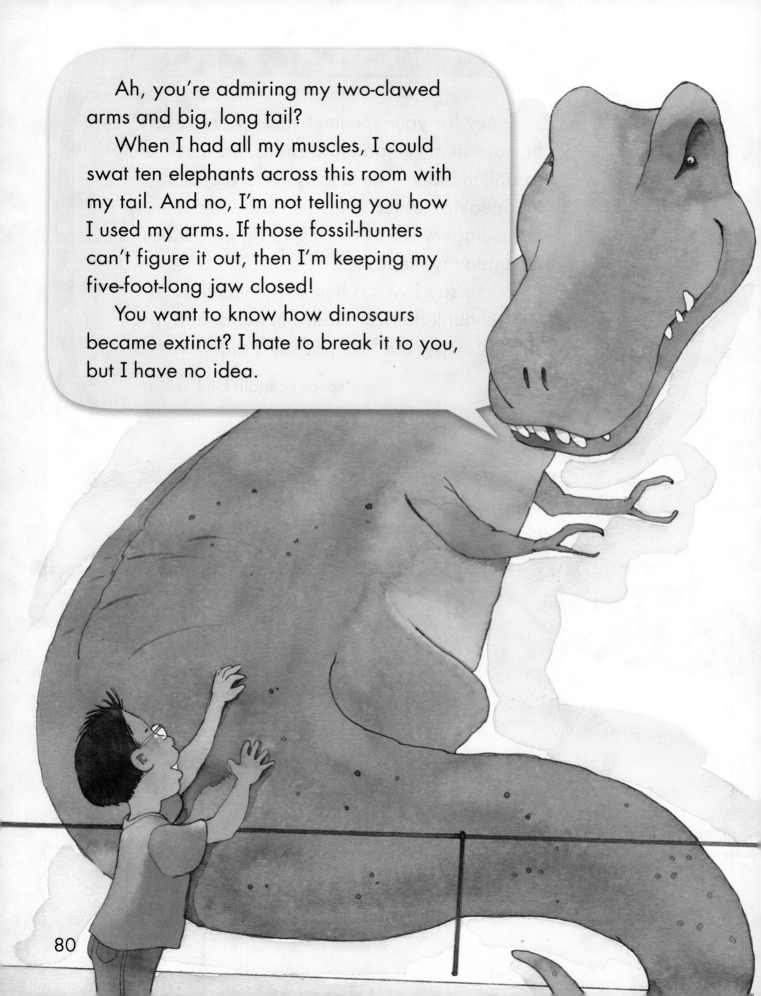

I was already taking a cozy nap in sandstone by then. And I would have stayed there too, if those dinosaur detectives didn't come poking at me with their chisels and drills.

I guess it's not so bad hanging out here. Lots of people come to admire me. I must say that I've kept my good looks!

Well, it's been nice talking to you. Maybe next time I'll tell you about the time I flipped over that *Ankylosaurus*.

Tyrannosaurus rex, or "the Tyrant lizard king," was one fierce dinosaur.

Some paleontologists think T-Rex ambushed and charged his prey. Others think that T-Rex was a scavenger.

T-Rex lived during the Cretaceous (krih-TAY-shuhs) era, the last age of dinosaurs before they became extinct.

4 you 2 Do

Word Play

Paleontologists excavate fossils from sandstone. How many words can you "dig up" by using letters from this word:

paleontologist

Making Connections

How was Maxwell's discovery like finding a treasure?

On Paper

When paleontologists discover a new dinosaur, they get to name it. Imagine you have discovered a new dinosaur. Describe what it looks like. Give your new dinosaur a name.

Possible answers to Word Play: stone, tools, site, goat, pal, log, pale

Making Music

Contents

Making Music

Let's Explore

84

Words 2 the Wise

Music and musicians affect us in different ways. As you read, think about how musicians are making music.

Let's Explore Music

It's a sunny afternoon in Mexico. People are gathered on the streets for a fair. Suddenly the sound of trumpets and guitars fills the air. A mariachi (mar-ee-AH-chee) band plays!

A small crowd gathers around a stage in India. Soft music chimes, and girls in long, colorful clothing move gracefully to the beat. They wear dangling bells on their wrists and ankles. Long braids hang down their backs.

Musicians in mariachi bands play trumpets, guitars, violins, and harps.

Dancers with long braids and jingling jewelry dance to Indian music.

In a big city, lights flash and cars zoom as people rush along the street. A man sits on the corner playing a saxophone. The jazzy notes of his song blend with the other city sounds.

People have made music since the beginning of time. Wherever you go, chances are you'll find music. What kind of music do you like?

In the United States, street performers entertain people.

Irish step dancers make music with the hard soles of their shoes.

In Africa, drums are a big part of traditional music.

HOMEMADE *Harmonies*

by Mitchell Banks

A bucket as a drum? A bottle as a flute? Sometimes the simplest items make the best sounds. This was the idea behind jug bands* and skiffle music.**

A jug is the main instrument in a jug band. The first jug bands formed around 1900 in the southern United States. These bands played blues, jazz, and folk music. They used a variety of instruments. Many were homemade.

---

*jug band a band that has a jug player and other homemade instruments

**skiffle music a style of folk music using homemade instruments

Skiffle music is like jug band music. Many people didn't have much money but still wanted to play music. So they made their own instruments.

Skiffle and jug bands play traditional instruments like the guitar, fiddle, and banjo. But they also make instruments from household items, including jugs, spoons, and combs. The sounds of these items work together to make great harmony.

The banjo helps create the special sound in skiffle music.

JAMMIN' JUGS

The most important instrument in a jug band is a jug. Playing a jug is similar to playing a flute or trumpet. They are all wind instruments. Wind instruments make sound by moving air through a tube.

To play your own jug, get an empty soda bottle. Blow *across* the opening in the top. Don't blow air *into* the bottle, or you will not make a good sound.

A bottle makes a perfect wind instrument!

This musician uses an old washboard to make music.

SCRUB OUT A TUNE

Another popular homemade instrument is the washboard. A washboard is a metal board with ridges on it. Long before washing machines were invented, people scrubbed clothes on washboards.

The washboard is a percussion (per-CUH-shin) instrument. Percussion instruments help mark the beat in music. Sound is made by hitting two objects together. Drums, chimes, and cymbals are other percussion instruments.

You might not have a washboard. But you might find one at a flea market or music store. To play it, you sit with the washboard between your knees. Drag a wooden spoon or brush up and down the board. What a nice "clean" beat!

Musicians use new washboards that hang around their necks.

A TASTY RHYTHM

Spoons can also be used as a percussion instrument. To play the spoons, make a fist. Place the handle of one spoon between your pointer finger and middle finger. Now hold the other spoon between your thumb and pointer finger. The bottoms of the spoon bowls should be back to back.

Hit the spoons against the palm of your opposite hand. They should click together. Each click is a beat. Try to play in harmony with another instrument.

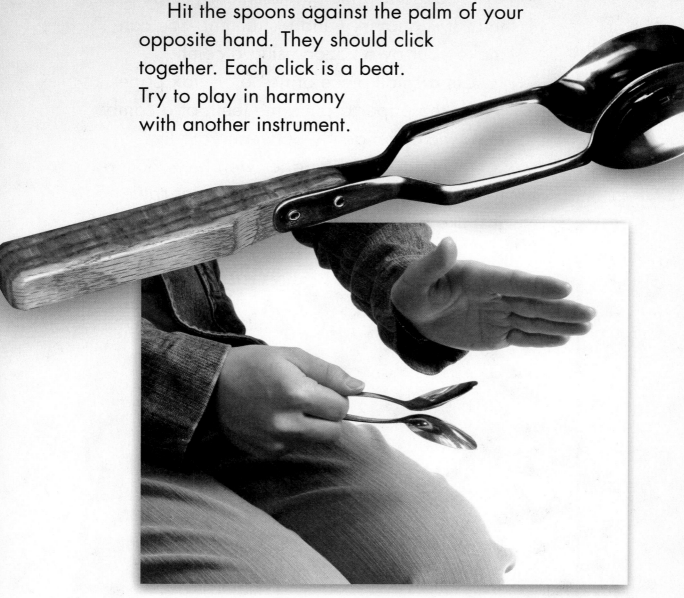

The trick to playing spoons is to keep a firm grip.

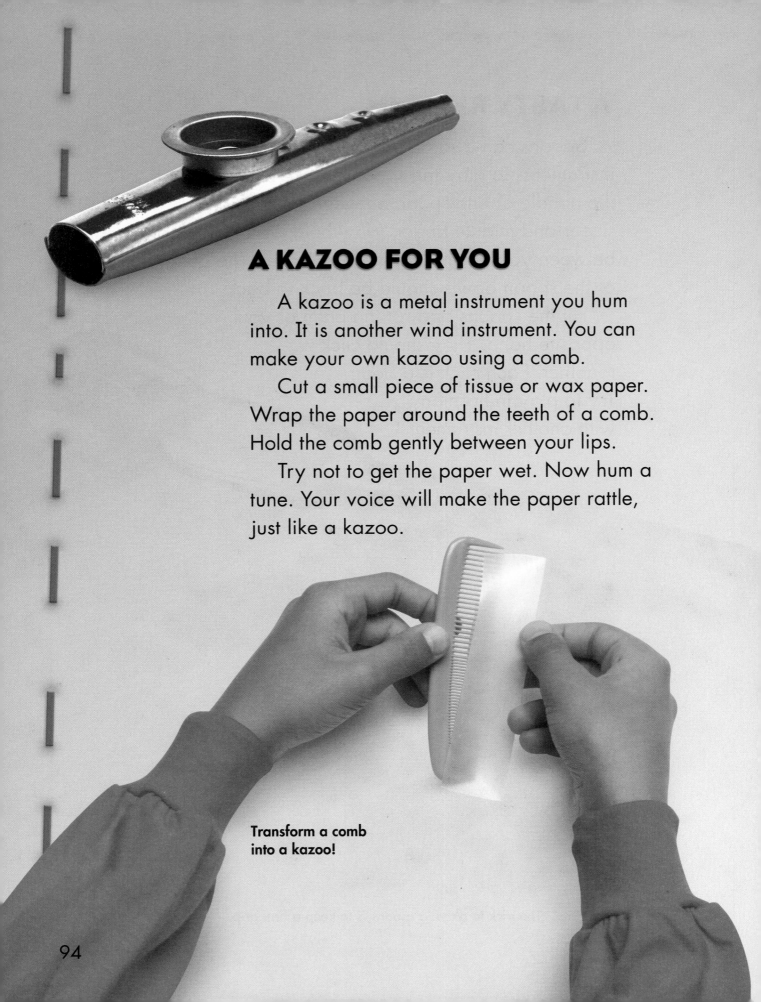

A KAZOO FOR YOU

A kazoo is a metal instrument you hum into. It is another wind instrument. You can make your own kazoo using a comb.

Cut a small piece of tissue or wax paper. Wrap the paper around the teeth of a comb. Hold the comb gently between your lips.

Try not to get the paper wet. Now hum a tune. Your voice will make the paper rattle, just like a kazoo.

Transform a comb into a kazoo!

INGREDIENTS FOR FUN

You don't need a fiddle or a banjo. Try a bottle, a washboard, some spoons, or a comb. By using these simple items, you can create great instruments. Now all you have to do is invite some friends over. You're ready to form your own jug band!

Homemade harmonies
are the best harmonies.

WHAT DO YOU THINK?
How can you make music without buying an instrument?

MIXING IT UP ★

BY MARGARET DIXON

Musicians want to share their music with others. They want people to hear their songs. How can musicians do this?

Performing a concert is one way. Fans come to hear musicians perform live. The crowds can be large or small. But no matter how big the crowd is, a musician can reach only one audience at a time with a concert.

Musicians can't be everywhere at once. They also can't have a concert every time someone wants to listen to their music. But they can reach a larger audience by making a recording!

Musicians record their music to CDs so that more people can enjoy their songs. Fans can listen to CDs as many times as they want.

Many musicians use a recording studio to record their music. Musicians can record their songs onto a CD in a studio.

Live music doesn't allow you to hear your favorite music every day!

There are recording studios all over the world. Many studios are small. They have simple equipment. Others are very large.

A recording studio has rooms with special equipment. These rooms are built so that no outside sound can get in and ruin a recording.

Musicians use microphones to record their instruments. Big instruments like drums need a lot of microphones. Smaller instruments like guitars need only one.

This musician is recording a song for her CD.

Once all the microphones are set up, the recording can begin! But making a CD is not easy. The volume on each instrument has to be just right. The drummer can't miss a beat. The piano player can't hit the wrong key. The singer can't forget the words! If the musicians make a mistake, it will ruin the recording.

Many things can go wrong! How do musicians make sure that their CDs are perfect?

Recording studios need lots of equipment to make music.

Many musicians record one instrument at a time. The drummer records the drums until every beat is perfect. Then the keyboard player records until every note is perfect. Each instrument is recorded separately until the sound is right. Then musicians mix them together to record a song.

This process takes time. Musicians make many changes to their songs to get them right. Sometimes little mistakes can become big problems.

Each of the instruments will be played until the recording is just right.

Recording each instrument separately can make planning easier. If a singer can't be at the studio when the rest of the band is ready, the recording can still go on. The rest of the band can still play their parts. The singer can record the vocals for the song later.

Musicians mix everything together on a machine called a mixing board. When the CD is played, it sounds like all the musicians played at the same time!

Musicians mix everything together on this machine to make a song for their CD.

Once the musicians record and mix the sounds of all their instruments, they make sure that the volume for each one is not too high or too low. If each part blends well, the song is finished.

But it takes a lot more than one song to make an album. Musicians have to make many songs. They spend months making sure that every song sounds just right.

We can buy CDs of our favorite music in stores.

Once all of the songs are ready, they are recorded onto a CD. Thousands of CDs will be made.

Radios can play the recordings from the CD. People can own the CD and listen to it whenever they want. With every CD, musicians find new fans and inspire more people!

What Do You Think?

Why do musicians record their music on CDs?

CDs allow fans to hear their favorite music any time.

A World of INSPIRATION

India.Arie

India.Arie won two Grammy Awards in 2002.

Name India.Arie
Country United States
Favorite instrument acoustic guitar
Albums *Acoustic Soul* (2001),
Voyage to India (2002),
Testimony: Vol. 1 (2006),
Testimony: Vol. 2 (2009)
Musical influences Stevie Wonder,
James Taylor, Bonnie Raitt

This four-time Grammy Award winner sings about love, faith, family, and inner strength. Her message inspires fans to take pride in who they are! Her songs encourage others to stand up for what they believe.

Anoushka Shankar

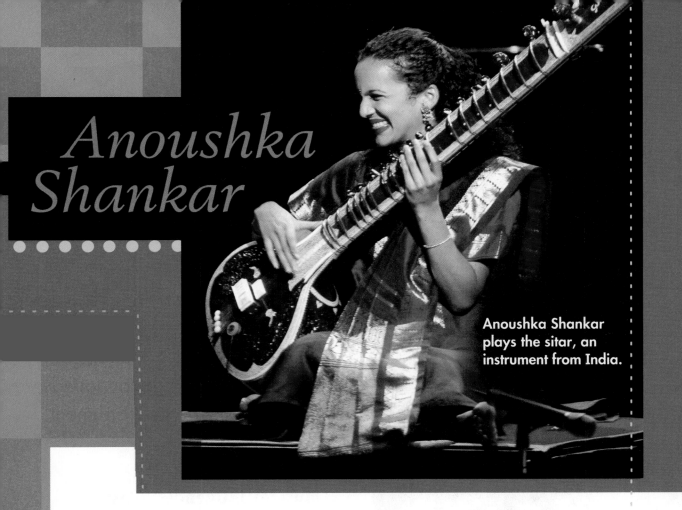

Anoushka Shankar plays the sitar, an instrument from India.

Name Anoushka Shankar (ah-NOOSH-kuh SHAHN-kar)
Country England
Favorite instrument sitar*
Album *Rise* (2005)
Biggest musical influence
Ravi Shankar (RAH-vee SHAHN-kar), her father

Anoushka began taking sitar lessons when she was seven years old. Her teacher was her father. Ravi Shankar is a famous sitar player. Anoushka creates Indian music for the world to enjoy. She is also a writer, an actress, and a conductor.

*sitar guitarlike stringed instrument with a long neck extending from a deep gourd

105

Habib Koite

Habib Koite uses African songs as a base for his music.

Artist Name Habib Koite (hah-BEEB ko-EE-tee)

Country Mali

Favorite instrument guitar Habib makes his guitar sound like a West African instrument called the *kora*.

Album *Baro* (2001)

Musical influences West African praise singers, Cuban music, and rap

Habib uses his music to speak out against injustice. In 2005 he went on a tour of the United States to raise support for farmers around the world.

Has a singer's voice ever made you feel chills run down your spine? Has music ever inspired you to sing along, write a poem, or even cry? If so, you are one of many people who has been touched by music.

Musicians entertain us. But they often have a message. The next time you hear your favorite song, listen to how the instruments and voices work together. These artists want you to also hear the message.

4 YOU 2 Do

Word Play

Every song is made up of beats. A beat is a pulse of music. Every word is made up of beats also. These beats are called syllables. How many syllables, or beats, are in the following words?

beat   skiffle   harmony

instrument   fiddle

Making Connections

How is homemade music like music made in a recording studio? How is it different?

On Paper

Think of an object at home that might make a good instrument. Describe it.

Illusions

Contents

Illusions

Words 2 the Wise

Special effects create illusions that help make plays and movies seem more real. As you read, think about how these illusions are created.

Let's Explore Setting

Costumes, lighting, scenery, props, and sound effects are the tools that create illusions for plays. These are the things that help bring a theater to life.

Directors use different ways to make plays and movies look real.

A play comes to life with the right costumes, scenery, and lighting.

the Stage

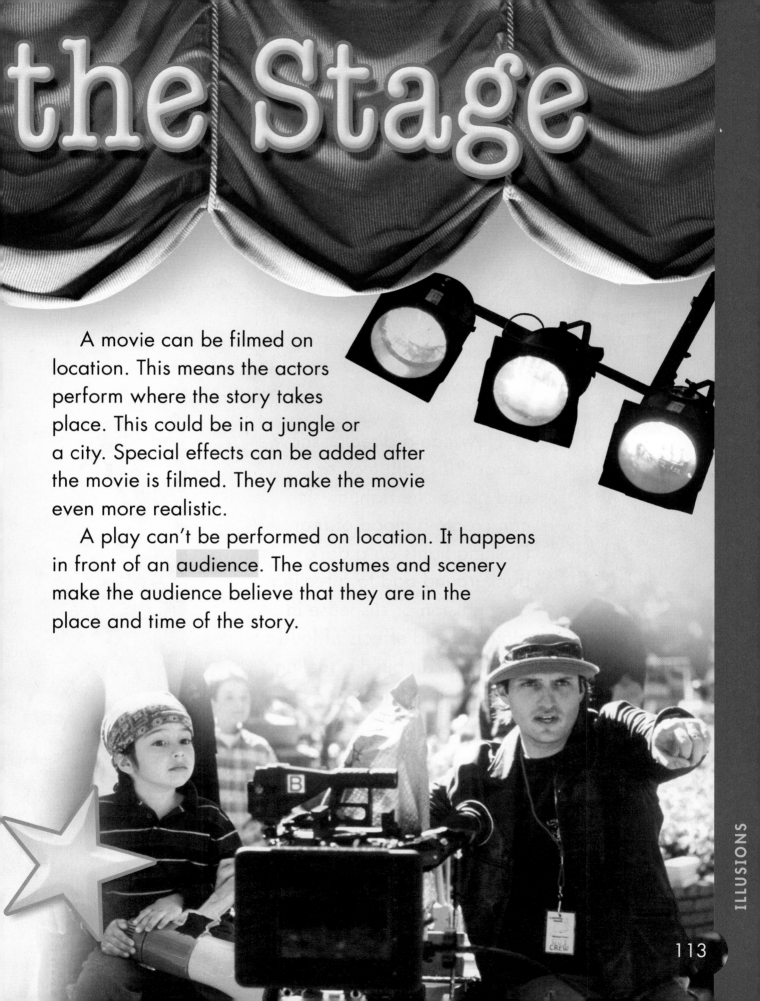

A movie can be filmed on location. This means the actors perform where the story takes place. This could be in a jungle or a city. Special effects can be added after the movie is filmed. They make the movie even more realistic.

A play can't be performed on location. It happens in front of an audience. The costumes and scenery make the audience believe that they are in the place and time of the story.

How can a director show danger? In both movies and plays, the right music can create a mood of fear. Flashing lights on a dark background add to a feeling of confusion or suspense in plays. Sound effects of loud footsteps can build a feeling of terror in movies.

In a play or movie, artists help create illusions. Artists paint scenes that look like real castles, oceans, or jails. They design and build bridges, buildings, or even carnivals right on stage.

The next time you watch a movie or play, think about how the set, special effects, and costumes make it seem real.

The Cirque du Soleil*

by Theresa Volpe

The theater has a soft orange glow as if a fire were burning. The performers seem to be hiding! They whisper to each other. The mood is mysterious. The audience looks around the theater, waiting for something to happen.

A prince and princess appear. Suddenly, arrows fly! A battle breaks out. Warriors leap into the air, swinging swords and doing back flips. The prince and princess run away.

*Cirque du Soleil SIRK doo so-LAY

Cirque du Soleil performers

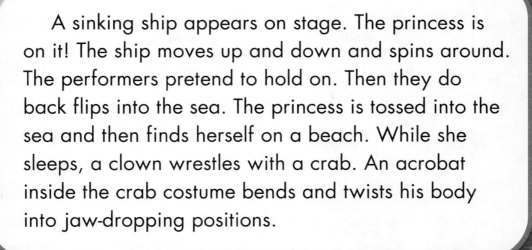

A sinking ship appears on stage. The princess is on it! The ship moves up and down and spins around. The performers pretend to hold on. Then they do back flips into the sea. The princess is tossed into the sea and then finds herself on a beach. While she sleeps, a clown wrestles with a crab. An acrobat inside the crab costume bends and twists his body into jaw-dropping positions.

The princess wakes up next to a giant crab!

What happens to the princess? The audience at a Cirque du Soleil show wants to know too. The show leaves everyone wanting more.

Cirque du Soleil is a circus, but not one with lions jumping through hoops. There are no animals. Cirque du Soleil is sometimes performed under a big tent, but what you see is not like anything you can see at a usual circus.

Here's a glimpse into how Cirque du Soleil creates these illusions.

Performers hang from silk ropes and perform a ballet.

Music in Motion

The sound effects that Cirque du Soleil creates are as unique as the acts. The music helps tell the story. It sets the mood and signals the performers. The music slows down or speeds up to match the performance.

The music is from around the world. First, it may sound like South African music. Next, it may sound like Spanish music.

Cirque du Soleil can be performed under a circus tent.

Cirque du Soleil music is performed live.

The singers might sound as if they're speaking a foreign language. They are speaking bits and pieces of words taken from many languages. These sounds become sound effects that help create mood.

The Stage and Equipment

Cirque du Soleil has illusions of danger and excitement. One show has a ring of fire. Another has a million-gallon pool of water. A floor rises and falls inside the pool. Water drains through holes so the surface is dry for performances.

The stage for this show is a pool that is twenty-five feet deep.

Characters don't just walk onstage in this show. They float! The show's guide stands in an upside-down umbrella that seems to glide across the water. This is an illusion. There is a motor that makes it move.

Even the show's equipment is unique. Cirque du Soleil invented something called the "fast track." The stage floor turns into a trampoline. Performers run, bounce, and do flips on the springy surface. But Cirque du Soleil uses traditional circus equipment as well.

The German Wheel is a giant hoop with a performer inside. He uses his strength to make the wheel spin and turn as he does difficult flips.

The Russian Swings send performers sailing through the air. They land feet-first on top of another performer's hands. A canvas wall catches soaring performers.

Dressed to Impress

A performer in a black and green lizard costume creeps and crawls along the stage floor. He stops to stare into the eyes of one individual in the audience. What is this creature's purpose? What does the audience imagine when they see the brilliant costumes and make-up?

Performers jump from swing to swing on the Russian Swings.

Bringing It All Together

Cirque du Soleil shows tell a story through the music and the performers. Costumes, make-up, and stages tell the story too. The combination works to create unbelievable illusions.

Costumes are designed for beauty and to work well with the performers' movements.

What Do You Think?

How do you think Cirque du Soleil is different from a traditional circus? How is it the same?

LIVE ON THE AIR!

by Clare O'Brien
illustrated by Jennifer Emery

The radio play ended. Mr. Gordon clicked the CD player off and turned to the class. "Open your eyes. What sound effects did you hear?"

"Rain," said Sara, "and footsteps."

"A train," said Mark.

Brandon hooted like the owl on the radio broadcast. He tapped the desk with his fingers while he whistled. "I heard an owl," he said, "and footsteps, *and* a train at the same time."

Mr. Gordon glanced at the clock and tuned the radio to WKDZ. When the song ended, D.J. Johnny Jam's voice announced, "Next month we will broadcast live from Eleanor Roosevelt Elementary School. Grade 5, Room 10, will put on a play for your listening enjoyment."

The class was excited. They had lots of ideas. What kind of play would they do? A scary play? A western? Or maybe a play set in outer space!

"How can we decide?" asked Jasmine impatiently.

"Well," said Mr. Gordon, "I'll play more clips of radio broadcasts from the 1930s and 1940s. Families didn't have televisions so they listened to radio shows."

After the last clip played, Mr. Gordon asked for comments.

"It will be impossible to make our play that good," said Tony. "We can't make those effects!"

"Not unless we can get a horse, a helicopter, and a rocket ship!" said Jasmine.

Mr. Gordon winked. "The radio stations don't have animals and aircraft!"

He took off his shoes and started tapping them on the desk like footsteps. First slowly, then quickly. Bam! He slammed the door.

"The character ran out because a monster was chasing him!" said Jasmine.

"Maybe he was chasing his dog," shrugged Luke.

"That's right! Sound effects are invisible to the audience," nodded Brandon.

"Like the crack of the bat at a baseball game," said Jasmine. "You don't need the bat, just something to make the same sound."

Brandon clicked his tongue and made a cracking sound. "Home run!"

"Exactly," said Mr. Gordon.

Then the recess bell rang.

"After recess we'll start working on the play," Mr. Gordon shouted over the noise.

"Brandon, please stay for a minute," said Mr. Gordon. "You would make a great lead soundperson. I'd like you to be in charge of finding items to make all the sounds we need."

Brandon smiled and nodded. His mind was already spinning with ideas. The play wasn't written yet. But when it was, Brandon would be ready.

The big day came quickly. D.J. Johnny Jam set up his equipment on the stage. "If you make a mistake, keep going," he said smiling.

Students helped set ordinary materials onto the prop table. There was also a coconut cut in half!

Brandon sat in front of his very own microphone. His two helpers got out the metal baking sheets and the watering can.

The D.J. yelled, "Action!"

Tony began, "It was a dark and stormy night . . ."

The sound effects crew went to work. Students shook the baking sheets. *Crash! Boom!* Rain and thunder roared. Brandon clapped coconuts onto the wooden board. *Clip, clop.* A horse galloped down the street.

Students couldn't take their eyes off the crew. The sound effects were great!

After the play, many listeners called the radio station. The audience wanted to hear the play again. They asked about new plays too. Room 10 would be busy. Live radio broadcasts were exciting!

What Do You Think?

How is performing a radio play different from performing a play an audience can see?

CREATING Special Effects

Before television, radios told stories. Since you couldn't see the actors, sounds were very important. Many sound effects were made with common household materials. Here's how you can create scenes through sound.

On a stormy night, it rains without stopping.

1 Use a thin, metal cookie sheet. Shake it. *Kaboom!* Thunder.

2 Place popcorn kernels in a pie pan. Shake the pan. Rain!

A poisonous rattlesnake slithers out from under the bushes. A mad rattler is ready to strike!

1 Place several grains of uncooked rice in the bottom of a small paper cup.

2 Tape a second cup on top.

3 Shake, shake.

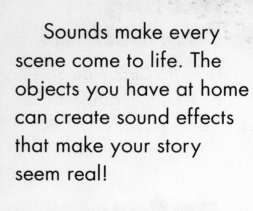

Sounds make every scene come to life. The objects you have at home can create sound effects that make your story seem real!

Turn plastic cups upside down and make the clip-clop sounds of a horse trotting down the road.

4 You 2 Do

Word Play

For each example below, tell which sound effect would make an audience member feel the emotion listed on the left.

Emotion	Sound Effect
1. fear	crying
2. sadness	clapping
3. excitement	door creaking

Making Connections

How do Cirque du Soleil and the fifth graders create illusions?

On Paper

Think of another sound effect you could create. What is it? How could you make it?

Glossary

au·di·ence (ȯ′ dē əns), *NOUN.* a group of people that is watching something or listening to something: *The audience liked the band that played on the street.*

beat (bēt), *NOUN.* a sound that repeats at a set time: *Joy liked listening to the beat of the drums.*

brain·storm (brān′ stôrm′), *VERB.* to come up with many ideas or solutions; to solve a problem: *The students brainstormed to come up with an idea for their science project.*

a in hat	ō in open	sh in she
ā in age	ȯ in all	th in thin
â in care	ô in order	ᵺ in then
ä in far	oi in oil	zh in measure
e in let	ou in out	ə =a in about
ē in equal	u in cup	ə =e in taken
ėr in term	u̇ in put	ə =i in pencil
i in it	ü in rule	ə =o in lemon
ī in ice	ch in child	ə =u in circus
o in hot	ng in long	

bril·liant (bril′ yənt), ADJECTIVE.

1 great or wonderful:
The singer gave a brilliant
performance.
2 having great intelligence:
She is a brilliant teacher.

broad·cast (brȯd′ kast′),

1 NOUN. a program on TV or radio: We watched the
President's broadcast from Washington, D.C.
2 VERB. to send out by TV or radio: Some stations
broadcast shows twenty-four hours a day. **broad·cast
or broad·cast·ed, broad·cast·ing.**

can·vas (kan′ vəs), NOUN.

1 a strong, heavy cloth
made of cotton:
Some tents are made
of canvas.
2 a picture that is painted
on the cloth:
The beautiful canvas was
hanging in the art gallery.
PL. **can·va·ses.**

Yellow and Gold, Mark Rothko

col·lec·tion (kə lek′ shən), *NOUN.* a group of things gathered from many places and belonging together: *Our library has a large collection of books.* *PL.* **col·lect·ions.**

con·cert (kon′ sərt), *NOUN.* a live musical show: *The band gave a free concert in the park.*

con·sid·er (kən sid′ ər), *VERB.* to think about something in order to decide: *Jack considered all the movie choices before choosing the space movie.* **con·sid·ered, con·sid·er·ing.**

a in hat	ō in open	sh in she
ā in age	ò in all	th in thin
â in care	ô in order	ŦH in then
ä in far	oi in oil	zh in measure
e in let	ou in out	ə =a in about
ē in equal	u in cup	ə =e in taken
ėr in term	ů in put	ə =i in pencil
i in it	ü in rule	ə =o in lemon
ī in ice	ch in child	ə =u in circus
o in hot	ng in long	

ef·fect (ə fekt′), *NOUN.* the feeling that is created by using objects in special ways: *Tilting a tube with sand in it makes a sound effect like rain.* *PL.* **ef·fects.**

e·val·u·ate (i val′ yü āt), *VERB.* to find out how well something is working: *We will evaluate the idea to see if it will work.* **e·val·u·at·ed, e·val·u·at·ing.**

ex·ca·vate (ek′ skə vāt), *VERB.* to uncover by digging: *Scientists have excavated many fossils of dinosaur bones.* **ex·ca·vat·ed, ex·ca·va·ting.**

ex·per·i·ment (ek sper′ ə ment),

    1 *VERB.* to test or try something out: *The cook will experiment with a new recipe.* **ex·per·i·ment·ed, ex·per·i·ment·ing.**

    2 *NOUN.* a test to find out something: *We did a science experiment to find out how electricity works.*

ex·press (ek spres′), *VERB.* to show something by your look, voice or action: *A smile expresses joy.*

ex·tinct (ek stingkt′),
    ADJECTIVE. no longer existing:
    Dinosaurs are extinct.

fa·mous (fā′ məs), *ADJECTIVE.* very well known: *Many people came to see the famous singer perform.*

fid·dle (fid′ l), *NOUN.* a violin:
    John played the fiddle with the jug band.

a	in hat	ō	in open	sh	in she
ā	in age	ȯ	in all	th	in thin
â	in care	ô	in order	₮H	in then
ä	in far	oi	in oil	zh	in measure
e	in let	ou	in out	ə	=a in about
ē	in equal	u	in cup	ə	=e in taken
ėr	in term	ů	in put	ə	=i in pencil
i	in it	ü	in rule	ə	=o in lemon
ī	in ice	ch	in child	ə	=u in circus
o	in hot	ng	in long		

fos·sil (fos′ əl), NOUN. a part or print of a plant or animal that lived a long time ago: *Fossils of dinosaurs that lived long ago have been found all over the world.*

gal·ler·y (gal′ ər ē), NOUN. a room or building used to show collections of pictures and statues: *Ben looked at the paintings of clouds at the art gallery.*

har·mo·ny (här′ mə nē), NOUN. using two or more musical sounds that go well together: *The two singers made great harmony during the concert.* PL. **har·mo·nies.**

il·lu·sion (i lü′ zhən), NOUN. something that looks different from what it actually is: *The mirror gave him the illusion of being very tall.*

in·stru·ment (in′ strə mənt), NOUN. something that makes music: *He can play the piano and two other instruments.*

in·ven·tion (in ven′ shən),

NOUN. something new that someone makes or thinks of: *The light bulb is a wonderful invention.*

live (līv), ADJECTIVE. not previously recorded on tape or DVD; broadcast during the actual performance: *They broadcast a live performance of the play.*

mur·al (myu̇r′ əl), NOUN.
a large picture painted on a wall: *The neighbors painted a mural on the side of the old building.*

pa·le·on·tol·o·gist (pā′ lē on tol′ ə jist), NOUN. a person who studies animal and plant fossils from prehistoric times: *The paleontologist studied the bones of the large dinosaur.*

a	in hat	ō	in open	sh	in she
ā	in age	ȯ	in all	th	in thin
â	in care	ô	in order	ᴛʜ	in then
ä	in far	oi	in oil	zh	in measure
e	in let	ou	in out	ə	=a in about
ē	in equal	u	in cup	ə	=e in taken
ėr	in term	u̇	in put	ə	=i in pencil
i	in it	ü	in rule	ə	=o in lemon
ī	in ice	ch	in child	ə	=u in circus
o	in hot	ng	in long		

per·form·er (pər fôr′ mər),
NOUN. someone who acts, sings,
or plays instruments in front of
people: *Singers, dancers, and
musicians are performers.*
PL. **per·form·ers.**

pre·his·to·ric (prē′ hi stôr′ ik), ADJECTIVE. belonging to times
before history was written down: *Dinosaurs lived in
prehistoric times.*

proc·ess (pros′ es or prō′ ses), NOUN. a set of steps in order to
achieve a goal: *What is your process for getting your
school projects finished on time?*

re·cord (ri kôrd′), VERB. to copy music, words, or pictures for
future use: *The singers can record music in the studio.*

sand·stone (sand′ stōn′), NOUN. a kind of rock that is made
mostly of sand: *Builders used sandstone instead of brick to
make our house.*

site (sīt), NOUN. the position or place of something: *The site for
the new school is across from the park.*

stu·di·o (stü′ dē ō), *NOUN.* a place where musicians make music: *The singer went to the studio to record a CD.*

style (stīl), *NOUN.* a way of painting, writing, composing, or building: *There are many different styles of painting at the art museum.*

the·a·ter (thē′ ə tər), *NOUN.* a place where people go to see movies or plays: *We saw the movie at the new theater.*

the·or·y (thē′ ər ē or thir′ ē), *NOUN.* an idea or opinion about something: *My theory is that the fire started from a candle.*

a in hat	ō in open	sh in she
ā in age	ȯ in all	th in thin
â in care	ô in order	ŦH in then
ä in far	oi in oil	zh in measure
e in let	ou in out	ə =a in about
ē in equal	u in cup	ə =e in taken
ėr in term	u̇ in put	ə =i in pencil
i in it	ü in rule	ə =o in lemon
ī in ice	ch in child	ə =u in circus
o in hot	ng in long	

Acknowledgments

Text

Every effort has been made to locate the copyright owner of material reproduced in this component. Omissions brought to our attention will be corrected in subsequent editions. Grateful acknowledgment is made to the following for copyrighted material.

54 The Authors Licensing & Collecting Society (ALCS) "The Paint Box" by E.V. Rieu from *The Flattered Flying Fish*. Used by permission of the Authors Licensing & Collecting Society Ltd on behalf of the estate of the late E.V. Rieu.

55 Dial Books for Young Readers, A division of Penguin Group (USA), Inc. "Genius" from *A Dime a Dozen* by Nikki Grimes, Copyright © 1998 by Nikki Grimes, text. Used by permission of Dial Books for Young Readers, a Division of Penguin Young Readers Group, a member of Penguin Group (USA) Inc., 345 Hudson Street, New York, NY 10014. All rights reserved.

Illustrations

Cover: Bonnie (Sam) Tomasello; **1, 26–29** Bonnie (Sam) Tomasello; **2, 6, 18–25** Bradley Clark; **11–16** Bill Petersen; **32, 54, 55, 95** Meg Aubrey; **58, 78–81** Elizabeth Allen; **58, 70–77** K.E. (Karen) Lewis; **67** Susan J. Carlson; **110, 124–131** Jennifer Emery.

Photographs

Every effort has been made to secure permission and provide appropriate credit for photographic material. The publisher deeply regrets any omission and pledges to correct errors called to its attention in subsequent editions. Unless otherwise acknowledged, all photographs are the property of Pearson Education, Inc. Photo locators denoted as follows: Top (T), Center (C), Bottom (B), Left (L), Right (R), Background (Bkgd)

Cover: (CR) Chris Farina/Corbis, (CL) Getty Images, (CR) Grant Faint/Getty Images, (CL) Jeff Haynes/Getty Images; **1** (CL) Getty Images; **2** (BR) Katarina Stoltz/Reuters/Corbis; **3** (CR) Hemera Technologies, (TC) Rough Guides/Alamy Images, (BR) Walter Meayers Edwards/Getty Images; **5** (BL) Getty Images, Iain Masterton/Alamy Images; **6** (CR) ©John Power, (TL) Getty Images; **7** (L) Getty Images; **8** (CL) Digital Art/Corbis; **9** (T) Jupiter Images, (CL) Science Photo Library/Photo Researchers, Inc.; **10** (BR) ©John Power, (Bkgd) Getty Images; **12** (Bkgd) Getty Images; **13** (CR) Hemera Technologies; **14** (Bkgd) Getty Images; **16** (Bkgd) Getty Images; **17** (TR) Brian Babineau/©John Power, (BR) Hemera Technologies; **30** (BL) Getty Images; **31** Stephen Simpson/Getty Images; **32** (BR) Dave Nagel/Getty Images, (TR) Deborah Van Kirk/Getty Images, (CR) Grant Faint/Getty Images, (TR) Richard T. Nowitz/Corbis; **33** (TR) Getty Images, (L) Tom Stewart/Corbis; **34** (L) Getty Images; **35** (C) ©2006 Artists Rights Society (ARS), New York/ADAGP, Paris/©Peter Willi/SuperStock, (L) ©Chuck Eckert/Alamy, (BC) A Basket of Oranges, Eloise Harriet Stannard (1829–1915)/Private Collection, ©Ackermann and Johnson Ltd, London, UK/Bridgeman Art Library, (B) Getty Images; **36** (CL) Deborah Van Kirk/Getty Images, (B) Getty Images, (B) Richard T. Nowitz/Corbis; **37** (CR) ©1998 Kate Rothko Prizel & Christopher Rothko/Artists Rights Society (ARS), New York/SuperStock, (B) Gail Mooney/Masterfile Corporation, (B) Getty Images; **38** (Bkgd) Getty Images; **39** (B) Bob Krist/Corbis, (TR) Francis G. Mayer/Corbis; **40** (TR) ©Steve Hamblin/Alamy, (Bkgd) Getty Images, (BR) SuperStock; **41** (TR) ©The Georgia O'Keeffe Foundation/Artists Rights Society (ARS), New York/Bettmann/Corbis, (BL) ©The Georgia O'Keeffe Foundation/Artists Rights Society (ARS), NY/©Christie's Images, New York, (TR, BL) Smithsonian American Art Museum, Washington, DC/Art Resource, NY; **42** (Bkgd) Getty Images, (B) Grant Faint/Getty Images; **43** (TR) Frank Siteman/Getty Images, (B) Tom Stewart/Corbis; **44** (B) David R. Frazier Photolibrary, Inc./Alamy Images, (Bkgd) Getty Images; **45** (T) Katarina Stoltz/Reuters/Corbis; **46** (B) Getty Images, (BL) ©Drivepix/Fotolia; **47** (BR) Dave Nagel/Getty Images; **48** (B) ©Jay Paul for ART 180; **49** (TC) ©Jay Paul for ART 180, (B) Getty Images, (CL) Hemera Technologies; **50** (T) ©Mary Elizabeth Meier, Getty Images, (L) Hemera Technologies; **51** (BR, B) Getty Images, (BL) Hemera Technologies, (C) Julie Lemberger/Corbis; **52** (T, CL, B) Getty Images; **53** (B) Getty Images; **56** (BR) Tom Stewart/Corbis; **57** (BL) Getty Images, Rough Guides/Alamy Images; **58** (CR) ©William Whitehurst/Corbis, (TR) Getty Images, (CR) ©Marc Hill/Alamy Images, (TR) Reuters/NewMedia, Inc./Corbis; **59** (TR) Getty Images, (L) Richard A. Cooke/Corbis; **60** (CR) ©DEA Picture Library/Getty Images, (TL) Ewell Sale Stewart Library/Academy of Natural Sciences; **61** (B) Reuters/NewMedia, Inc./Corbis; **62** (TR) ©William Whitehurst/Corbis, (BC) Bernardo Gonzalez Riga/epa/Corbis, (Bkgd) Getty Images; **63** (B) W. Cody/Corbis; **64** (TL) Dave King/Getty Images, (TC, CL, Bkgd) Getty Images; **65** (B) Getty Images, (T) ©Marc Hill/Alamy Images; **66** (TC) Francois Gohier Pictures, (Bkgd) Getty Images; **68** (T) Brooks Walker/National Geographic Image Collection, (Bkgd) Getty Images; **69** (TC) epa/Corbis, (BR) Getty Images; **82** (BL) Getty Images, (R) Richard A. Cooke/Corbis; **83** (Bkgd) Dex Image/Getty Images; **84** (BR) ©Reuters NewMedia Inc./Corbis, (TR) Goncalo Diniz/Alamy Images, (CR) Hemera Technologies, (CR) Pwpix/Alamy Images; **85** (BL) Lukas Creter/Getty Images; **86** (BL) Bill Bachmann/Index Stock Imagery, (BR) Goncalo Diniz/Alamy Images; **87** (BL) ©Scenicireland/Christopher Hill Photographic/Alamy, (BR) Bruno Morandi/AGE Fotostock, (TR) Getty Images, (TC) Jeff Greenberg/AGE Fotostock; **88** (Bkgd) ©Hemera/AGE Fotostock, (TL) Getty Images/Getty Images, (CL) Hemera Technologies; **89** (TC) Owen Franken/Corbis, (R) Redferns Music Picture Library/Alamy Images; **91** (CL) Bob Krist/Corbis, (BR) Hemera Technologies; **92** (L) Daniel Templeton/Alamy Images, (BR) David Redfern/Redferns, (TL) Jonathan Knowles/Getty Images; **93** (C) Getty Images; **95** (BR) Getty Images/Getty Images; **97** (B) Chritopher Bissell/Getty Images; **98** (BL) ©Dave Nagel/Getty Images, (Bkgd) Getty Images; **99** (B) Pwpix/Alamy Images, (CR) Redferns Music Picture Library/Alamy Images; **100** (L, C, BR) Hemera Technologies; **101** (B) Paul Arthur/Getty Images; **102** (L) Blasius Erlinger/Getty Images, (Bkgd) Getty Images; **103** (B) Alex Mares-Manton/Getty Images; **104** (CL) Quasar/Starmaxinc/NewsCom; **105** (TC) ©Reuters NewMedia Inc./Corbis; **106** (CL) ©Didier Ruef/Aurora Photos, (TR) Redferns; **107** (TL) Frank Micelotta/Getty Images, (B) John Van Hasselt/Corbis; **108** (R) Lukas Creter/Getty Images; **109** (Bkgd) Getty Images, (Bkgd) Gustau Nacarino/Corbis; **110** (TR) Dimension Films/Shooting Star International; **111** (BR) Getty Images, (L) Robert Daly/Getty Images; **112** (Bkgd) G.K. & Vikki Hart/Getty Images, (B) Michael S. Yamashita/Corbis; **113** (B) Dimension Films/Shooting Star International, (TR) Michael Pole/Corbis; **114** (TL) Michael Pole/Corbis; **115** (C) Adan Woolfitt/Corbis; **116** (BR) Bruno Vincent/Getty Images, (BL) John D McHugh/Getty Images, (BC) Paul Hackett/Reuters/Corbis; **117** (Bkgd) AP/Wide World Photos; **118** (Bkgd) Nicolas Asfouri/Getty Images; **119** (BR) Chirstinne Muschi/Reuters/Corbis, (C) Michael Newman/PhotoEdit; **120** (BR, BC) Chris Farina/Corbis; **121** (Bkgd) David Hancock/Getty Images; **122** (BC) AP/Wide World Photos; **123** (CL) Bruno Vincent/Getty Images, (CR) John D McHugh/Getty Images; **132** (Bkgd) ©Joel Sartore/National Geographic Image Collection, (TL) Dave Rudkin/©DK Images; **133** (BL) Christopher Furlong/Getty Images, (TR) Walter Meayers Edwards/Getty Images; **134** (Bkgd) Getty Images, (TR) Robert Daly/Getty Images; **135** (TC) Jeff Greenberg/AGE Fotostock; **136** (BR) ©1998 Kate Rothko Prizel & Christopher Rothko/Artists Rights Society (ARS), New York/SuperStock, (TR) Frank Micelotta/Getty Images; **137** (C) Bill Bachmann/Index Stock Imagery; **138** (CR) Richard A. Cooke/Corbis; **139** (CR) Dex Image/Getty Images, (TR) Reuters/NewMedia, Inc./Corbis; **140** (C) Grant Faint/Getty Images; **141** (CR) ©Mary Elizabeth Meier, (TR) Hemera Technologies; **142** (TR) Getty Images; **143** (TC) Redferns Music Picture Library/Alamy Images.